Lewis Reifsneider Harley

A History of the Public Education Association of Philadelphia

Lewis Reifsneider Harley

A History of the Public Education Association of Philadelphia

ISBN/EAN: 9783337005597

Printed in Europe, USA, Canada, Australia, Japan

Cover: Foto ©Thomas Meinert / pixelio.de

More available books at **www.hansebooks.com**

A HISTORY

OF THE

Public Education Association

OF PHILADELPHIA

BY

LEWIS R. HARLEY, PH. D.

LATE HONORARY FELLOW IN THE UNIVERSITY OF PENNSYLVANIA

WITH AN INTRODUCTION

BY

EDMUND J. JAMES

PROFESSOR IN THE UNIVERSITY OF PENNSYLVANIA

PUBLIC EDUCATION ASSOCIATION
PHILADELPHIA
1896

CONTENTS.

INTRODUCTION.

The last fifteen years have constituted an important period in the history of public education in Philadelphia. During this time many improvements have been made and a number of movements inaugurated which are destined to result in still further progress.

The establishment of the principle of supervision, as incorporated in the superintendency and in the institution of supervising principalships;

The opening of two manual training high schools, and the complete vindication of the wisdom of the movement for manual training afforded by the success of these schools;

The introduction of manual training and sewing into the lower schools;

The recognition of the necessity of training the taste of the pupils as well as their intellects, shown, among other things by the growing attention to school-room decoration;

The introduction of the principles of household training— notably cooking in the City Normal School for Girls;

The separation of the Normal from the Girls' High School and the adequate development and equipment of each of these great institutions;

The passage of a compulsory school law;

The development of facilities for the training of teachers at the University;

The increase of opportunities for the training of teachers in vacation time in connection with the University Extension Summer Meeting;

The greatly increased interest and pride of the community in our public school system stimulated by such exhibitions of the work of pupils as that held in Horticultural Hall in May, 1888—surely all these taken together constitute most substantial progress.

The time is rapidly coming when Philadelphia will take as much pride and interest in its public schools as does Boston or Chicago; when the last vestiges of that harmful feeling so long prevalent in this city that the public schools are for the poor, will have disappeared—a feeling which can be easily explained on account of the origin of the public school system; * but a feeling which is certainly in these days no longer justified.

In the great work of these last years, the Public Education Association can fairly claim to have played an important part. It has aided all the movements for the better; it has itself instituted and carried through some of the most important. In doing this, it has followed worthily in the footsteps of many preceding associations of similar aim; for nearly every great

---

* Cf. C. S. Bernheimer, " Public Education in Philadelphia." With an Introduction by Edmund J. James. Published by the Public Education Association, 1896.

improvement in our public school system—nay even the establishment of that public school system itself—has been brought about by the efforts of some voluntary association of public spirited citizens, in sympathy with, though not a part of, the public school system.* This is true even though the first thought of the improvement may in some cases have been owing to men engaged in the system either as teachers or as members of school boards. What the Association has done and tried to do is told more fully in the following pages by Dr. Harley, and on page 38 is given a brief summary of the directions in which it has been active.

The work is, however, not by any means all done. Eternal vigilance is the price of success. The existence of some such association as this is necessary to the highest welfare of the schools. Standing outside of the school system, this body is always watching its workings, willing to lend a helping hand whenever an old abuse is to be abolished or a new improvement introduced—ready to throw the weight of its influence in favor of those forces which make for progress in our schools and to ward off all attacks upon their existence or efficiency, whether they come from openly avowed enemies of the schools or from those still more dangerous enemies who, under the guise of friendship and sympathy, seek merely to use the schools to advance their own private or political ends.

The Association may rightly ask all public spirited citizens to aid in this work.

---

* Cf. C. S. Bernheimer, " Public Education in Philadelphia."

The immediate task before the Association is:

(1) To assist in the movement to reform the present system of educational administration in the city. For six years past the Association has labored to persuade the community and the Legislature that the relations between the local and central school boards are not such as they should be. The existing plan involves irresponsibility, wastefulness and inefficiency. The powers of the Central Board should be strengthened at least to such a point as to enable it to exercise a thorough and efficient control over the equipment of the school houses, the character of the teaching and the assignment of pupils;

(2) To assist in enforcing the new compulsory school law which, from present indications, is destined to remain largely a dead letter unless public attention is thoroughly aroused to its importance;

(3) To aid in the development of the rapidly growing interest in the training of children along esthetic, moral and physical, as well as intellectual, lines;

(4) A continuance in its persistent efforts to arouse and concentrate public interest in the schools; for after all, the rapid and permanent improvement of the public school system must rest upon an intelligent and pervasive public interest in the schools themselves.

In publishing this brief account of the work of the Public Education Association, it is proper to refer to the distinguished services of Dr. James MacAlister to the cause of public education in this city; first as Superintendent of Schools, and later as President of the Drexel Institute, which, under his direction, has become a most valuable supplement to the existing agencies in this community for public education. Nor should we members of the Association forget the earnest and self-sacrificing labors of Miss Charlotte Pendleton, who first suggested the organization of the Association, as its Secretary during the twelve years in which it has been most active. It is not too much to say that without her important and continuous labors the work of which we have reason to be proud could not have been accomplished.

The Association should, moreover, hold in special honor the memory of two of its earliest and most active members : Edward T. Steel and Mrs. J. Dundas Lippincott. To their unwearied efforts the Association owes much of its success, and for their devotion to the interests of public education in this community every Philadelphian should be grateful.

EDMUND J. JAMES,
Chairman.

University of Pennsylvania,
January 1, 1896.

THE PUBLIC EDUCATION ASSOCIATION OF PHILADELPHIA.

EARLY HISTORY.

The desirability of improving the school system of Philadelphia has given rise to a number of voluntary associations, which have been actively engaged for several years in urging reforms and promoting the development of the schools in various ways. Among the most active of these organizations has been the Public Education Association of Philadelphia.

This association, like some of its predecessors, grew out of charity work.* Its source was the Committee on the Care and Education of Dependent Children of the Society for Organizing Charity. When the charity organization was founded in 1880, it appointed five general committees to formulate and direct its work. Miss Pendleton was one of the five original members of the Committee on the Care and Education of Dependent Children, and at the first meeting of the Committee, she was appointed chairman of the sub-committee. At this meeting, held November 27, 1880, the following resolution was adopted :

Resolved, that a sub-committee of five be appointed to study and report upon compulsory and industrial education.

The chair appointed the following committee: Miss Pendleton, Miss Hallowell, Mrs. Gillingham, Jos. S. Whitney and Professor R. E. Thompson.

The work of the sub-committee was subdivided, Miss Pendleton taking up the question of Compulsory and Industrial Education, and Miss Hallowell the Care of Dependent Children. Out of Miss Pendleton's work grew the Public Education Association ; out of Miss Hallowell's the Sub-Primary Society.

---

*Cf. C. S. Bernheimer, "Public Education in Philadelphia," Public Education Association, 1896.

At the monthly meeting of the Assembly Committee of the Philadelphia Society for Organizing Charity, held January 8, 1881, to consider compulsory and industrial education great interest was shown in these subjects by those present. Addresses were made by Judges Pierce and Tourgec, Professor R. E. Thompson and Mr. Charles G. Leland. Speaking of compulsory education, Judge Tourgee said that he had positive convictions on the subject, as his life had been spent where education was conspicuous for its absence. As a mere police preventive against pauperism, he insisted that every citizen should know at least the "three R's," and that the right of a nation to impose education is simply the right of self-defence in another form.

Before the committee had finished their report, it was realized that here was a field of great usefulness, and that it should be extended beyond the limits of dependent children to the whole field of public education.*

At a meeting of the Assembly March 7, 1881, Miss Charlotte Pendleton read the report on compulsory and industrial education under the four heads : (1) what is taught in the public schools; (2) what should be taught; (3) how many children are out of school; (4) why are they out.

Miss Pendleton reported that in 1879 there were 103,567 pupils in the city schools :

High School, ... 495 boys.
Normal School, ... 975 girls.
School of Practice, ... 307 "
Grammar schools, . . 7,243 boys and 7,838 "
Consolidated schools, . 3,869 " 3,551 "
Secondary schools, . 12,724 " 13,585 "
Primary schools, . . 27,138 " 25,842 "

The grade of the schools was not uniform owing chiefly to the lack of a superintendent. Drawing was the only subject

---

*The development was very similar to that in the early days regarding free schools themselves. Cf. Bernheimer's "Public Education in Philadelphia."

given to develop dexterity of the hand. More than 21,000 children were out of school. At least 5000 had been refused for lack of accommodations. A large number were illegally employed in factories, besides which there were many derelict and neglected children. Miss Pendleton's report contained a clause suggesting the foundation of an education association, and the meeting appointed a special committee, consisting of Mr. George L. Harrison, Mr. James S. Whitney and Miss Pendleton, to take charge of the recommendation. The committee consulted such persons as Mr. Charles Francis Adams, Jr., Dr. John D. Philbrick, Miss Lucretia P. Hale, Mr. J. P. Wickersham, Mr. Edward T. Steel and Mr. Charles G. Leland. The queries submitted to them were:

1. Do you approve of compulsory education?

2. If you disapprove, how do you propose to fill the schools?

3. If you approve, do you recommend the public school system, or a semi-industrial system?

4. Do you approve of drawing, the use of tools and sewing in the schools?

5. Do you approve of Froebel's Kindergarten System?

6. At what age should the education of the child by the State begin?

7. Do you approve of State schools of handicraft, or of subsidies from the State to such schools?

While differing in regard to many points, there was unanimity of opinion in matters of practical application. These gentlemen also favored the formation of an education association. A committee was appointed, consisting of Mr. James S. Whitney, Mr. Charles G. Leland, Mr. Edward Shippen and Miss Pendleton, to prepare rules and by-laws. The special committee of the Assembly reported that steps had been taken to form the association and asked to be discharged.

Thus the persons who had met to discuss the advisability of forming it became the nucleus of the Public Education Association. The Committee on Rules made a report at a meeting held early in May, 1881, and under the rules adopted at this meeting the following executive committee was elected:

To serve one year { MRS. ROBERT HARFORD HARE,
MISS PENDLETON,
PROFESSOR BARKER.

To serve two years { MR. ROBERT E. PATTISON,
MISS MEREDITH,
MR. CHARLES G. LELAND.

To serve three years { MR. JAMES S. WHITNEY,
MISS IRWIN,
MR. E. COPPÉE MITCHELL.

RULES OF THE ASSOCIATION.

The following rules were adopted at this meeting:

1. The name of the Association shall be the Public Education Association of Philadelphia.

2. The object of the Association is to promote the efficiency and to perfect the system of education in Philadelphia; by attracting general attention to its errors and defects; through appeals to the local authorities and to the Legislature when needful, and through such other means as may from time to time be deemed expedient—becoming thus a medium for the expression of public opinion—and especially to take such measures as may be feasible to bring under instruction the thousands of children now growing up in ignorance.

3. The Association shall consist of those persons whose names are appended to this paper, and of such others as may from time to time be elected, as hereinafter provided.

4. The management of the Association shall be vested in an Executive Committee, to consist of nine members, chosen by ballot by the Association. The first election shall be held at the time of the adoption of these rules, and the committee then elected shall, at its first meeting thereafter, divide itself by lot into three classes of three members each. The term of the first class shall expire on the third Monday of the following January, and those of the second and third classes

one and two years later respectively, and at each stated annual meeting the Association shall elect three of its members to serve for three years as members of said committee.

5. Members of the Executive Committee, whose terms have expired, may be candidates for re-election, and in case of failure to hold the election at the time stated, the members whose terms have expired, shall continue to act as members of the committee until the election shall be held.

6. The Executive Committee shall elect a Chairman, Secretary and Treasurer; shall fill all vacancies in its body and make all rules for its management; it shall hold stated meetings at least once in three months, at which it shall receive and vote upon the names of all persons proposed for election to membership in the Association, and it shall make a written report to the Association at each stated annual meeting of its transactions for the previous year.

7. The stated meetings of the Association shall be held annually on the third Monday of January. Special meetings may be called by the Chairman of the Executive Committee at his discretion, and shall be called by him when requested, in writing, by five members of the Association.

8. These rules shall be amended only by a two-thirds vote of the members of the Association present and voting at a general meeting. *Provided*, That notice of the change proposed be given in the call for the meeting at which such action is to be taken.

The following circular was also issued stating the objects of the Association.

CIRCULAR

OF

The Public Education Association of Philadelphia.

It is the object of this Association to promote the efficiency and to perfect the system of public education in Philadelphia, by which term is meant all education emanating from, or in any way controlled by, the State. They purpose to acquaint themselves with the best results of experience and thought in education, and to render these familiar to the community and to their official representatives, that these may be embodied in our own public school system. They seek to become a centre for work, and a medium for the expression of opinion in all matters pertaining to education; as, for instance, the appointment of superintendents; the compilation of school laws; the kindergarten in connection with public education; manual instruction—how much is desirable, and what it is practicable to introduce into the public-school system; the hygiene of schools; the adequate pay and the better qualification of teachers; and, above all, to secure, as far as possible, universal education, by bringing under instruction that large class, numbering not less than twenty-two thousand children, who are now growing up in ignorance in this city.

These objects the Association hope to attain through appeals to the local authorities, and to the Legislature, and by such other means as may be deemed expedient.

The management of the Association is vested in an Executive Committee, consisting of nine persons, elected by ballot from among members of the Association—three members of said committee retiring each year; these vacancies to be filled by ballot, and the retiring members to be eligible for re-election.

Annual membership dues $2.00.

THE SUPERINTENDENCY OF THE SCHOOLS.

The objects of the Association are stated in the above circular, but before giving a detailed history of the organization, it may be of interest to state the general condition of public education in Philadelphia. The school system of Philadelphia is supported by local taxation, and the general administration of the system is vested in a Board of Education appointed by the Judges of the Courts of Common Pleas, and serving without pay. Each ward also has a Board of Directors, elected by the people, and serving without compensation. In

1882, the number of pupils in the public schools was 105,541 with an average attendance of 94,145. The number of pupils out of all schools, public and private, at that date was estimated at 28,000.

At that time nobody knew how all the children were taught in the 400 school houses. The local boards did not know, for they did not visit the schools regularly, or if a director here and there did stray into a school occasionally, he had no means of judging whether it was worse or better than other schools, or whether it was good at all. A superintendent was as much needed for the schools as a mayor for a city. In 1882 New York had one superintendent and seven assistant superintendents, and Boston and St. Louis had each superintendents, while the schools of Philadelphia, with one-third as many pupils as the whole State of Massachusetts, were without any adequate supervision. At that time the school laws were very meagre and inadequate. The question relating to the Kindergarten and Manual Training was, however, attracting attention in Philadelphia, and the question of universal education began to excite increasing interest.

The Association naturally took up that work with which the members were occupied when the Association was formed. Action was at once taken concerning matters connected with industrial education and the appointment of a superintendent of public schools. Early in 1882, a Sub-Committee of the Association conferred with the Board of Education, with a view to securing the concerted action of the Board and the Association in an effort to procure an appropriation from Councils for the appointment of a superintendent of schools, and to consider the advisability of urging upon Councils the establishment of a school for instruction in the use of tools and studies related thereto. At a meeting of the Board of Education, April 11, 1882, a by-law was adopted constituting the office of superintendent and assistants, and subsequently, the City Councils made an appropriation of $15,000 for their salaries for 1883. On March 12, 1883, Professor James MacAlister, of Milwaukee, was elected superintendent.

The Public Education Association did not of course originate the idea of a city superintendent of schools. Other cities had appointed superintendents years before. Buffalo appointed a superintendent of schools as early as 1837, and in 1839 Providence established the office. Cleveland, Ohio, elected a "manager of schools" in 1844, and Springfield, Mass., followed in 1845. In the decade between 1850 and 1860, the office of superintendent was created in many cities. But the school system of Philadelphia was, for many years peculiar, for up to 1883 it was the only system in a large city without a superintendent. The work of the Public Education Association, in aiding to establish the office, consisted in the interest it aroused by the holding of meetings and lectures; by the study of educational systems and questions, and the agitation of the subject in the columns of the city papers.

SEWING IN THE SCHOOLS.

As early as 1878, Miss Charlotte Pendleton, the first Secretary of the Association, suggested a collateral branch of intellectual training, for the purpose of training the hand as well as the brain. She favored a public school of trades and industry corresponding to the common and high schools of our present system, for the purpose of replacing the present system of imperfect training by apprenticeship. Speaking editorially of the theory, the *Evening Telegraph* said that the subject touched upon is an important one, and deserves to be discussed in all its bearings. The *Telegraph* could not agree with Miss Pendleton's views as to organizing trade schools in connection with the common schools, as it would be too much like paternalism, and it contended that all the government could do was to furnish elementary instruction. Referring to the same subject, Governor Hartranft said in one of his messages: "It is impossible to read the industrial history of the country without being struck with the decline of the system of apprenticeship, the decadence of skilled labor, and the rapid increase of common day laborers.

The work of the schoolmaster must undo the work of the demagogue, and the State supplant the bigoted organizations of labor with industrial schools and workshops."

One phase of this work was taken up as soon as the Public Education Association was formed. Miss Pendleton at the first meeting of the Association recommended that sewing should be taught in the Normal School. The next year this was done, and in 1885 instruction in sewing was introduced as a regular branch of the curriculum in the public schools. Instruction is given to the girls in all the grades above the primary. Special mention should be made of the work of Miss Lydia A. Kirby, in organizing the teaching of sewing.

MANUAL TRAINING.

The Association was active from the start in urging upon Councils the establishment of a manual training school. Early in 1882, the Secretary of the Association corresponded with Professor Ordway, vice-president of the Massachusetts Institute of Technology, in reference to the subject of manual training. Referring to this subject, Professor Ordway wrote as follows :

"MASSACHUSETTS INSTITUTE OF TECHNOLOGY,

"BOSTON, Mass., January 2, 1882.

"*Dear Friend:*—The instruction in carpentry is of direct use to those who have to work in wood, because the woodworking tools—the saw, the plane, the chisel, the draw-knife, the hammer, the square, the rule and the line—are used in many trades. One who has had this practice may become a house carpenter, a ship carpenter, a cabinet maker, a wheelwright, a carriage builder or a millwright.

" The wood turning and pattern making extend the range to these very important branches.

" Though we do not at present include wood carving in our course, we may say that one who has gone through with carpentry and wood turning, having had at the same time instruction in drawing, is well prepared to learn the art of carving.

2

"The foundry work which the students do gives them a good beginning in the business of the iron, brass and bell founders.

"Blacksmithing is essential for the boiler maker, the nail and bolt maker, the chain maker, the cutter and the iron bridge builder.

"The vise work is important for locksmiths, gunsmiths and watchmakers, and of course for the general machinist.

"The engine lathe work is that of machinists, and is a good preparation for taking care of any kind of machinery.

"We ought to have a paint shop and a department of soldering and brazing, but we are at present short of room. I hope we may some time get more land and add these things.

"Our course makes no provision for the textile manufactures, for the work of the saddler, the printer, the bookbinder, the engraver, the bricklayer, the plasterer, the tanner, the currier, the glassblower, or the chemical trades. But the general training of the hand and the eye gives a dexterity and accuracy which lie at the foundation of all good and profitable work.

"In all the arts, the hands must be used as well as the brain, and the handling of tools gives a more practical control of the muscles than gymnastic exercises, or no exercises at all.

"Nature indicates the use of tools to the growing boy, who must have at least his jack-knife. It is important that right habits be formed, and that the boy should use his muscles to some purpose instead of working at random. Training in the accurate use of tools affords a good mental discipline aside from its every-day practical use.

"Yours, very truly,

"John M. Ordway."

A sub-committee was at once appointed by the Association to confer with the Board of Education and urge the adoption of the manual training system as practiced in the Massachusetts Institute of Technology. During November and December, 1883, the following course of lectures, relating to the various phases of Industrial Education was given under the auspices of the Association :

" Public Education," by James MacAlister, Superintendent of Schools, Philadelphia.

" The Old and The New Education," by G. Stanley Hall, Lecturer on Pedagogy at Harvard University, and on Psychology at the Johns Hopkins University.

" Handwork in Education," by Professor John M. Ordway, Massachusetts Institute of Technology.

" The Financial and Administrative Aspects of Public Education," by Professor E. J. James, University of Pennsylvania.

Early in 1884, the Board of Education decided to establish a manual training school, and asked Councils for an appropriation for that purpose. At a meeting of the Executive Committee of the Public Education Association, October 29, 1884, the following memorial to Councils was prepared:

" The Public Education Association of Philadelphia, having learned of the application of the Board of Public Education for an appropriation for the establishment of a school for manual instruction, desire to express to Councils, through the Finance Committee, their earnest hope that such appropriation be made, and to urge, very briefly, some considerations in its favor.

" 1. If our public schools are to educate the community into the most useful citizenship, they will not do it by a partial and one-sided course, which reaches them through books and lectures only. Every man is the better educated if he knows how to work with his hands, whether he is to earn his livelihood thereby or not.

" 2. If our public schools are to fit pupils for self-supporting employments, their direct tendency should not be altogether to prepare for clerkships and similar positions, where the pen is the only implement used. Besides overcrowding these branches of labor, the inclination of the pupil is educated away from handicrafts, and those who would enter these find themselves not at all prepared for them.

" 3. This preparation cannot be had in shops since the different trades are now so divided into specialties, each of which is carried on on a large scale, particularly in large cities, that employers do not consider it their interest to train workmen in the rudiments which are common to most of them ; but these rudiments can be learned in schools and better than in workshops.

" 4. It need not be feared that such instruction will be experimental. Many such schools have been carried on for years in Europe, and now supply our shops with ready workmen, to the exclusion of our own boys. The considerations here presented have recently led to the establishment of similar schools in this country at Boston, St. Louis, Chicago Baltimore and other cities ; none of them having so large a manufacturing population as Philadelphia. In this city the Spring Garden Institute has shown what can be done by a private school, and Girard College has followed in the same path, under the direction of one department of the city government.

" We would add that teaching of this kind for boys is as justly part of a public school course as sewing, already introduced, is for girls, and would call your attention to a petition from large manufacturing firms of this city, addressed to the Board of Education, in April last, praying for the introduction of manual education in our schools.

" Respectfully submitted: James S. Whitney, William W. Justice, Philip C. Garrett, Committee on behalf of the Public Education Association."

Councils appropriated $7500 for the establishment of a school for manual instruction, and the Philadelphia Manual Training School was opened in September, 1885, with about one hundred and twenty-five pupils.

COOKING IN THE SCHOOLS.

When sewing was introduced, in 1881, into the Normal School, the Association upon the suggestion of Miss Pendleton expressed its desire to work out in the Normal School a system of instruction in the elements of household economy and related studies holding the same relation to the education of girls as instruction in the use of tools held to the education of boys. As sewing proved to be so successful, it was next proposed to establish a cooking school. At a meeting of the Executive Committee of the Association, February 9, 1885, it was resolved that a committee of three be appointed to confer upon the introduction of cooking into the Normal School. There were a number of conferences on the subject with the Committee of the Board of Education, and Miss Julia Corson, of New York, was invited to give demonstrations in the teaching of cooking. Great interest was shown in this subject by many of the most prominent people in Philadelphia. On January 8, 1886, Mrs. J. Dundas Lippincott opened her residence for a concert by amateurs for the benefit of the Public Education Association Cooking Fund, and a considerable sum was realized. Early in 1887, the Board of Education decided to place cooking in the Normal School to take the place of mythology. Two rooms in the basement were given for the purpose, and the Association paid for the plant. The Association also volunteered to contribute $1500 to meet the expenses of the school in cooking for the session of 1887–88. On December 12, 1888, the Association voted to guarantee to the Board of Education the cost of a teacher of cooking for one year, the cost of said teacher not to exceed $1000. The amount actually required was $800. In 1889, the Association contributed $955, and in 1890, $742.45 toward the cooking classes. The report of the Executive Committee of the Association for 1889 contains the following reference to the subject of cooking:

"The cooking schools which you have in turn supported until their expediency should be demonstrated, have increased in favor and usefulness. The city will assume the last of these in September, and until such time we shall require an additional sum of $500, if it be your pleasure to continue your work in this direction. The report of the Treasurer will give you the exact amount of your appropriations to these objects." The introduction of cooking into the schools was successful from the start. In 1888, one of the city papers, referring to the subject, said :

" Cooking is now half a year old in the Normal School, but seven years will not be needed to carry this new branch of domestic economy through the schools. Begun by private effort, the work of one fall has shown that cooking can be taught in the highest department of our city instruction without interference with the regular course, without using more room than was already at the service of the school, and with the addition of training in a field which fits for all the broad work of life. The slow swing of educated women away from the home and to the shop, the store and the office is, rightly or wrongly, the dread of the day. Nor is it strange, if, after training girls in all but what they would most need as wives and mothers, a bent toward doing in life what school had put first should show itself."

EXHIBITION OF SCHOOL WORK.

At the annual meeting of the Public Education Association, February 13, 1888, Hon. Geo. W. Hall laid before the meeting the following memorial addressed to the Board of Education, suggesting the propriety of holding a general public exhibition of the manual work of all kinds done in the public schools, including kindergarten, sewing, manual training, art work, drawing, designing and such other branches as can be properly exhibited in some central place during the spring months :

MEMORIAL.

PHILADELPHIA, February 13, 1888.

To THE BOARD OF EDUCATION.

Gentlemen :—The Public Education Association of this city have watched with great interest the various steps taken by your honorable body for the introduction of industrial training into the public schools. It is with great satisfaction that they have noticed the adoption of the Kindergartens, the introduction of sewing as a branch of instruction, in the girls' schools, the establishment of the Manual Training School, the reorganization and improvement of the Industrial Art School, and the opening of the experimental cooking class in the Girls' Normal School, as well as the general revision which the courses of instruction have undergone, with a view to rendering them not only better adapted to develop the intelligence of the children, but more practically useful in the business of life.

The Association is of the opinion that all these steps have met with the cordial approval of the people, and that they have been the means of arousing an unusual degree of interest in the public mind upon the subject of public education.

It seems to us that nothing is more vital to the improvement and prosperity of the public school system than an intimate knowledge on the part of the parents and the general public of the work carried on in the schools.

The exhibitions of sewing which have been held in the girls' schools during the past two years, and the opportunities which have been afforded them from time to time for seeing the work done in the Manual Training School have given great satisfaction.

With a view to bringing the people more fully into contact with the school work, and arousing a still wider interest in the schools, the Association beg to suggest to your Honorable body the propriety of holding a general public exhibition of the manual work of all kinds done in the public schools, including kindergarten, sewing, manual training, art, industrial work, drawing, designing and such other branches as can be properly exhibited in some central place during the coming spring months. The Association feels assured that such an exhibition would be gladly welcomed by the people, and would confer an opportunity for showing the substantial progress made in the schools in the past few years. We have been informed that arrangements can be made for such an exhibition without interfering with the regular school work of the pupils.

The Association understanding, however, that no public funds are available for this purpose, beg to say to your Honorable body that we will gladly bear whatever expense may be incurred in making this exhibition.

The Association, therefore, asks the attention of your Honorable body to the propositions herein recited, and will take great pleasure in conferring on the subject with any committee which it may be your pleasure to appoint.

WILLIAM W. JUSTICE,
Chairman of the Executive Committee.
WILLIAM W. WILTBANK,
Secretary.

The above memorial was adopted, and directed to be forwarded to the Board of Education by the Secretary. A special committee was appointed by the Board of Education to consider the proposed exhibition. Superintendent MacAlister suggested that it should begin on May 8 and continue four days. All kinds of school work should be exhibited under the five departments of Manual Training, Industrial Art, Kindergarten, Central High School and Girls' Normal School. Horticultural Hall was secured as the place of holding the exhibition. The exhibition opened under the most favorable circumstances, and it included the following branches:

I. Pupils' work.

II. Drawings and photographic views of the school buildings.

III. An exhibit of the supply department of the Board of Education.

IV. An historical exhibit.

V. Statistical statement of the educational system of the city.

VI. An exhibition of school work representing the practical operation of the following departments:

    1. Manual Training School.

    2. Industrial Art School.

3. Sewing Classes.
4. Kindergartens.
5. Cooking Classes.

VII. An exhibit showing the relation of the public schools to the other educational institutions of the city, in which public school scholarships are held.

The exhibition was a success. The most notable feature was the presence of classes under instruction. Eager spectators crowded about the drill of the Kindergarten, the little seamstresses using their needles intelligently and skillfully under the verbal direction of a teacher; the Normal School Cooking Class, the Industrial Art Classes and the busy workshops of the Manual Training School. Eighty thousand visitors passed through the gates from the opening to the close of the exhibition. Many of whom came from other parts of the country.

On May 11, President Smith, of Common Council, sent a letter to President Steel, of the Board of Education, urging him to use his influence to prolong the exhibition until the end of the next week, but this was not feasible, as the hall had been rented for other purposes. Telegrams were also received asking that the exhibits might be sent to San Francisco to be displayed at the exhibition in connection with the meeting of the National Teachers' Association in July; and also that they might be sent to the Industrial Exhibition at Melbourne in August, at the expense of Melbourne. It was felt, however, that the life of the exhibit was the working classes, not the numerous interesting specimens of work, and it was not thought advisable to exhibit the accomplished work without the educative method. The Public Education Association had offered a sufficient sum to cover the expenses of the exhibition in Horticultural Hall, and did this with a contribution of $2,216.56. In 1889, the Association contributed sufficient funds to enable the Board of Education to send an exhibit of the work of the Manual Training School to Paris. The work of this school was in advance of all competing American exhibits.

Manual Training High School for Girls.

In 1888, the Public Education Association took up another important phase of Industrial Education. Miss Pendleton presented a memorial to the Association, which was adopted, and a petition was sent to the Board of Education to establish a manual training high school for girls. The Association agreed to guarantee the rent of a building for the proposed school for three years. The project was approved by the Manual Training Committee of the Board of Education, endorsed by the New Century Club and the Working Women's Club, but on May 1, 1890, the Committee of the Board of Education deemed it inexpedient to accept the proposition for the reason that the Board had no funds to be applied to such a project.

The Kindergarten.

The Sub-Primary School Society,* organized for the purpose of establishing kindergartens in the city, invited the co-operation of the Public Education Association in bringing this subject into public notice. The Association, at an early date, collected a number of books, pamphlets, reports, etc., relating to the subject, and it was a part of the original intention to gather a little library of educational works, of interest to kindergartners. In 1884, there were twenty-seven kindergartens under the care of the Sub-Primary Society, and in 1886, the Board of Education assumed control of these schools, Councils appropriating $15,000 to enable the Board to make the start.† The next year, the Association appointed

---

* The active force in this society was Miss Anna Hallowell, to whose self-sacrificing labors Philadelphia education owes so much.

† This was brought about by an agitation in favor of public assumption of the Kindergartens begun by the Sub-Primary School Society. A public meeting was held in 1886, at which Dr. Edmund J. James delivered an address on the "Relation of the Public School to the Kindergarten," which was immediately printed by the Society, and contributed no little to accomplishing the end in view. Cf. Bernheimer's "Public Education in Philadelphia."

the following Committee on Kindergartens: W. W. Justice, Mrs. Hare, Mrs. Mumford, Philip C. Garrett. The report of the Executive Committee of the Association for 1887 says :

" We are anxious to make your Standing Committee on Kindergartens efficient in that important field. Mr. William W. Justice, who was a manager of the Sub-Primary School Society, which organized these admirable schools, is Chairman of this Standing Committee, and any members who are interested in this important work will kindly report to him. This is the only city in the country in which these valuable infant schools have been satisfactorily incorporated into the public school system. The zeal and judgment of the Sub-Primary School Society and the public spirit of the Board have contributed to this enviable result. It is not too much to claim for our city that the place in the front rank which we now occupy in public education is due to the wisdom, zeal and forbearance which have enabled the regularly constituted Official Board and private associations to work together for the common interest of public education. Long may this harmony exist to the infinite profit of the city ; for both are essential to good government under our institutions."

The work of Miss Constance Mackenzie in organizing kindergartens is deserving of special mention.

THE BOARD OF EDUCATION.

A leading object of the Public Education Association was to secure a reform in the administration of the city schools, by effecting a unification of the governing body.

After consultation with members of the Board of Education and of the Committee of One Hundred and others, the Association determined, in the interests of a more uniform and systematic oversight of the schools, to endeavor to have introduced in Mr. Bullitt's municipal reform bill a clause enlarging the powers of the Board of Education, and abolishing the boards of directors elected in the wards. The Association, backed by other influences, persuaded the Committee of One

Hundred to take up the matter. The draft of a clause, favored by President Steel, of the Board of Education, was submitted to the Legislative Committee of the Committee of One Hundred, but met with some objections. It proposed to do away entirely with the sectional boards, and to empower the Board of Education to appoint ward managers in each of the sections, and to provide competent superintendents for each group of schools. The serious objection was pointed out that as the members of the Board of Education are appointed by the courts, if the popular election of directors is denied, the direct control of the public schools by the people will be entirely destroyed. It was suggested that it might be well to have the Board of Education chosen electively by the people; but some were of the opinion that the character of the Board would deteriorate by such mode of selection. The Bullitt bill failed to provide for any reform in the control of the schools, and it is thus reviewed by the *Evening Star*, March 14, 1883 :

" The newly prepared bill for the better government of cities of the first class makes provision for much needed reforms in all the old municipal departments, and arranges for the creation of such new ones as the Department of Public Safety, Public Works, Charities and Corrections, but in regard to the Department of Public Education it has only a line and a half thus : Article 8, section 1, ' The Department of Education shall continue as now established by law.' "

Sectional school boards occupied a large share of attention at the fourth annual meeting of the Public Education Association on January 26, 1885, when the following resolutions were adopted :

" *Resolved*, That it is the deliberate judgment of this Association that the advance of public education in Philadelphia is grievously retarded by the imperfect system of control of the public schools now existing; that the interests of this community demand a radical change in this system, which shall include the appointment of numerous assistant superintendents to co-operate with and act under the direction of the

Superintendent of Public Schools, and the abolition of the local school boards, and the vesting of the powers of disbursing money and appointing and removing teachers and otherwise controlling the public schools of this city in the Board of Public Education; that all merely local and artificial divisions should be abolished both in the management of the schools and in the appointment of the members of the Board of Public Education, so that the interests of the whole community may always be kept in view and the system of education treated as a unit, sub-divided as convenience may require, and not as a mass of separate divisions, each independent of the other and subject to no common control such as exist at the present time.

"*Resolved further*, That this Association and its individual members will not rest satisfied until these measures are accomplished and will use their utmost endeavors to carry them through."

In 1885, when the bill changing the method of selecting the Board of Education from the Judges to election by popular vote was before the Legislature, the Association sent up a vigorous protest, and in 1887, when the proposition was introduced into the Legislature to abolish the Board of Education, the Association took active steps to defeat the measure, and at a meeting, April 18, 1887, the following resolutions were adopted:

"*Resolved* I. That this Association, while fully sensible that the organization of the public school system needs revision, considers that the bill now before the Legislature, so far from having this tendency, is calculated to increase rather than diminish whatever evils there may be both of localization and centralization, and hopes that before any legislation is undertaken on the subject thorough and careful examination shall be given to the whole question.

" II. The Association takes this occasion to call the attention of the Legislature to the necessity of the revision of the school sections, which have not been altered for thirty-three years, and which are not at all now in proper relation to the school population of the city.

" III. That the subject be referred to the Committee on Law to make such suggestions to the Legislature as may be in accordance with the views of the Association—and otherwise to act as they may deem proper."

The Association from the start strongly urged compulsory education, in order to bring the unfortunate classes into the schools, and in 1889, when the Riter Bill was before the Legislature, it received the cordial support of the Association. On March 21, 1889, the Executive Committee of the Association prepared the following memorial to the Legislature :

" The Public Education Association of Philadelphia approves and endorses the purpose of the bill now before the Legislature of Pennsylvania, known as the Riter Bill, for a compulsory system of education of children, so far as that bill is designed to secure an attendance at school.

" The provision of the first section of that bill relating to penalties does not meet the approval of this Association. No penalty in excess of two dollars per week as a maximum is deemed advisable, and in conformity with Pennsylvania law there should be no minimum.

" It is respectfully submitted to the General Assembly that it is the sense of this Association that a system of compulsory education is of the first importance in a State founded on universal suffrage ; and that the public welfare will be advanced by its adoption at this session in a comprehensive and well-considered code.

" Experience has shown the value of like enactments in other States and countries ; and the fact that Pennsylvania is not in front in this essential reform justifies those who advocate it in an urgent request that the bill be taken up for action at an early day."

The Public Education Association was active from the start in urging a reorganization of the Girls' High and Normal School. It was organized in February, 1884, for the special purpose of preparing teachers for the public schools. The crowded condition of the school and the demand for more advanced professional culture for teachers led the Public Education Association to urge that the High School and Normal departments be separated into two distinct schools. The attention of the Board of Education was directed to the matter, and on February 15, 1887, a committee of the Board recommended the organization of a girls' high school to relieve the Normal School. This was accomplished early in 1893. The school, as now organized, has three distinct courses of study. *First.*—A Classical Course, intended for those pupils who enter the school to acquire merely a higher education, or for the purpose of fitting them to enter college. *Second.*—A Business Course, to fit young women for clerks, or the various departments of business or trade. *Third.*—A General Course, to prepare pupils to enter the Normal School.

President Steel, of the Board of Education, in February, 1891, requested the Secretary of the Public Education Association, William W. Wiltbank, to prepare an Act of Assembly to be presented to the Legislature for adoption, which should provide a system of reorganization of the school department of the first district of Pennsylvania. A statute was accordingly prepared by Mr. Wiltbank. Hon. Charles A. Porter introduced the bill in the State Senate, and the Public Education Association, at the annual meeting, April 21, 1891, adopted resolutions approving the action of Senator Porter.

The energetic action of Mr. Steel and several other public-spirited citizens of Philadelphia secured a considerable amount of public attention for the proposed reform, and led, among other things, to a public meeting held at the Academy of Music May 4, 1891. This meeting was large and enthusiastic, and resolutions were adopted, urging that the local boards be abolished, and that the control of the schools be vested in one central board having complete authority over all questions relating to public education.

There were urgent representations made to the committees of the Legislature at that time, and a large delegation of citizens went to Harrisburg for a conference with a Committee of the Legislature there having the proposed bill in charge, and urged upon that body its favorable consideration and adoption.

This act was not passed by the Legislature. It was lost, we are informed, by a very small majority.

In 1893, the Public Education Association also took steps to procure the passage of the statute. In this instance, however, prominent men of the Legislature were in doubt as to a proper plan for the reorganization of the school department and declined to advocate that one which the Association had in view rather than some others presented to their attention by other bodies. The important question then arising was whether or not the Board of Education should comprise men of independence and position as private citizens, to be beyond the control of the municipal authorities, or whether there should be a director of public schools, etc., etc. The questions raised were too serious, and the difference of opinion too marked to make it practicable to secure any legislation at that session.

There was a joint meeting of the members of the Public Education Association and the Civic Club at the rooms of the Art Club, March 3, 1894. At that meeting an address entitled "Some Suggestions of Reform in the Public School System of Philadelphia" was delivered by Herbert Welsh, and Miss Pendleton read a paper on the "Unification of the School System." Dr. Edmund J. James, chairman of the Public Education Association and Mrs. Cornelius Stevenson, president of the Civic Club, also delivered addresses. The sentiment of the meeting was overwhelmingly in favor of an abolition of the local school boards as the first step to further improvement of the public school system.

Early in March, 1894, certain members of the Civic Club requested that the Executive Committee of the Public Education Association appoint a sub-committee to meet them in private conference in order that some plan might be formed, if practicable, for the renewal of the public interest in the proposition that the school department of the First District be reorganized, according to the plan exhibited by the Act of Assembly prepared by the Public Education Association in 1891. A meeting was accordingly called for Tuesday, April 3, 1894, at the residence of Mrs. J. Dundas Lippincott, and was well attended. There were representatives of the Civic Club and the Public Education Association present, and addresses were made. On motion of Miss Pendleton it was resolved that a committee be appointed by Mrs. Lippincott, who was then in the chair, to report upon the subject of legislation to be proposed to the General Assembly at its next meeting; the committee to have power to add to their number, and the present appointment to comprise five members of the two bodies, the additional number to be ten. This resolution was carried. Mrs. Lippincott appointed on that committee, Mr. William W. Wiltbank, Mr. Theodore Etting, Mr. Herbert Welsh, Mrs. Mumford and Miss Pendleton. Mr. Theodore Etting was appointed chairman. Mrs. Cornelius Stevenson, the president of the Civic Club, and Dr. E. J. James, the chairman of the Executive Committee of the Public Education Association, were added to that committee. This committee acted up to some time in the autumn of 1894, and later reported progress to its principals.

Subsequently the Act of Assembly, quoted at length below, was drawn by the Secretary of the Public Education Association, W. W. Wiltbank, and efforts were made to secure its passage at the session of the Legislature held in 1895.

The bill read as follows:

AN ACT

To provide for the organization of a Department of Education in cities of the first class and defining the powers and duties of the Board of Education herein provided for and repealing all laws or parts of laws inconsistent herewith.

SECTION I. Be it enacted by the Senate and House of Representatives of the Commonwealth of Pennsylvania in General

3

Assembly met and it is hereby enacted by the authority of the same that it shall be the duty of the Judges of the Courts of Common Pleas having jurisdiction in cities of the first class on or before the Fifteenth day of December One thousand eight hundred and ninety-five to appoint under their hands and under the seal of the said court a Board of Education comprising twenty-one persons residents of the city wherein the appointment is made, and it shall also be the duty of the said judges on or before the Fifteenth day of December in each year after the year One thousand eight hundred and ninety-five to appoint in like manner seven persons rèsidents of the city wherein the appointment is made to serve as members of the said Board of Education for the term of Three years commencing on the First Monday of January then next ensuing : And the said judges shall fill vacancies occasioned by removal resignation death or other cause by appointment made in like manner for the remainder of the term of the person or persons in respect of whom by removal death resignation or other cause the vacancy has been made.

Sec. 2. The said Board of Education shall serve without pay and shall organize on the first Monday of January One thousand eight hundred and ninety-six by the election from its own members of a president and other officers in its discretion and shall proceed to determine by lot the terms of service of the twenty-one persons appointed as in the foregoing section provided for so that seven of the said persons as determined by lot shall serve for one year from the first Monday of January One thousand eight hundred and ninety-six : other seven of the said persons as determined by lot shall serve for two years from the first Monday in January One thousand eight hundred and ninety-six : other seven of the said persons as determined by lot shall serve for three years from the first Monday of January One thousand eight hundred and ninety-six. The said Board of Education shall on the first Monday of January in each year thereafter organize and elect from its own members a president and other officers in its discretion and shall meet at least once in every month except July and August.

SEC. 3. The said Board of Education shall have all the powers of the Board of Education of the First School District of Pennsylvania as heretofore created and shall divide the city into school districts for convenience of organization and administration, and appoint a superintendent of schools, assistant superintendents and teachers and all other employees and shall have power to remove the same and shall determine upon the character of schools which shall comprise in addition to the common schools a Normal School for the education of teachers and such other special schools as the Board may from time to time deem it proper to organize and maintain. They shall also maintain sub-primary schools and night schools at proper seasons in each school year. They shall determine the number and location of school houses which shall be erected established and maintained in each of the said school districts and shall limit the expense of erecting establishing and maintaining the same. They shall provide for the maintenance and repair of school property and purchase such books and supplies as they shall deem necessary. They shall have the general superintendence and entire administration of all the schools in the said city and shall make such rules and regulations for their own government and the government of the schools as may be proper with power to appoint suitable men or women as local boards of visitors who shall serve without pay and whose duty shall be defined by the Board of Education. They shall keep accounts, and shall approve and certify the warrants necessary for the purchase of supplies and for the payment of costs of repair and maintenance and of the salaries of all salaried employees. They shall make an annual report of the administration of their office of the statistics of the schools and of their accounts to the Mayor and Councils of the said city.

SEC. 4. From and after the passage of this act no person shall be appointed by the Board of Education hereby created to the position of teacher in any one of the public schools of cities of the first class until such person shall have been duly qualified for the position contemplated by an examination under the authority of the said Board of Education which qualification shall be evidenced by a certificate made and attested by the superintendent of schools and approved by the said Board; *Provided*, however, that all teachers in the employ of the present school authorities in the cities of the first class at the time of the passage of this act shall be deemed to be eligible for their several positions without further examination and that all outstanding certificates of qualification have the same effect as if issued under the provisions of this Act.

SEC. 5. All appropriations of money which but for the provisions of this act would be applicable to public school purposes in cities of the first class are hereby made available to the Board of Education hereby created and all legal obligations outstanding in boards of controllers directors of public schools or other State organizations for public education in cities of the first class are transferred to the said Board of Education and boards of school controllers and directors heretofore created in cities of the first class are hereby abolished from and after the first Monday of January, One thousand eight hundred and ninety-six.

SEC. 6. Each of the said cities of the first class after a conference with the Board of Education hereby created acting by committee or otherwise shall annually levy a tax which in its discretion shall be deemed sufficient in the coming fiscal year for the maintenance of the schools in the said city and for the construction renting repair and other needs of the school buildings. The fund thus raised shall be subject to the order of the said Board of Education to be by it drawn upon by warrants duly approved and certified by the said Board of Education ; *Provided*, that nothing in this act shall be construed to authorize the said Board of Education to bind the said city for any debt unless created by virtue of the provisions of this act and payable out of the said fund or tax to be levied as aforesaid.

Sec. 7. All laws or parts of laws inconsistent with the provisions of this act are hereby repealed.

OTHER WORK OF THE ASSOCIATION.

In 1892 and 1893, the subject of a school census was before the committee. The necessity for a census of the children of Philadelphia arose from the fact that many children of the legal age were without the benefits of an education, and quite a number were unable to find accommodation in the public schools. A committee of the Association made an arrangement with the authorities of the Department of the Interior at Washington, in the Census Bureau, to obtain the tables of the census of 1890, showing the statistics of education in this State. An effort was also made to secure the co-operation of the Executive Department of Philadelphia in taking a census by the aid of the police force, and the sum of $250 was appropriated for this purpose.

In 1891 the Association appropriated the sum of $250 toward the establishment of a Chair of Pedagogy in the University of Pennsylvania, which was followed by a sufficient appropriation by the University to establish such a professorship, beginning with the autumn of 1894. The first incumbent was Professor Martin G. Brumbaugh. Thus, the Association gave the stimulus to the introduction of a needed element into the educational system of the city. The wisdom of this step is already demonstrated, as many teachers from the city and the surrounding country are taking advantage of the excellent courses in Pedagogy offered by the University.

Following the same line of work, the Association in 1893 appropriated the sum of $200, as a contribution toward the establishment of summer courses in Pedagogy for the benefit of the public school teachers of Philadelphia. These lectures were given in connection with the summer meeting held during the month of July, 1893, at the University of Pennsylvania, under the auspices of the University Extension Society. The lectures on Pedagogy have become a permanent feature of the summer meetings of the Extension Society, and at present

State Superintendent, Dr. N. C. Schaeffer, is at the head of a movement to offer extensive courses in Pedagogy at the summer meeting in 1896.

The Public Education Association has also taken considerable interest in æsthetic training in the schools. In 1893 the sum of $100 was contributed for the purchase of engravings, photographs, busts, etc., to be exhibited in the rooms of the Girls' Normal School; but as yet the Association has proceeded cautiously and has contributed moderately, in order that further information and experience may determine whether or not this course is expedient.

The Public Education Association has had a busy career of fifteen years. It has been a constructive period in educational work in Philadelphia, and the Association has seen the following results accomplished:

I. The institution of the department of superintendence, with the increase of force by which the efficiency of this department has been largely augmented and thoroughly organized.

II. The selection of a superintendent.

III. The introduction of sewing into the curriculum of the Normal School, and its more recent introduction, based upon the success of the earlier experiment, into the lower grades of schools, by which twenty-five thousand girls were, in 1887, receiving regular, systematic instruction in needlework.

IV. The universal acknowledgment that the most complete and satisfactory exhibition of this work ever made in the country was the exhibit of the sewing done in the public schools of Philadelphia made in the spring of 1886, at the Industrial Exhibition at New York.

V. The institution of the Manual Training School.

VI. The reorganization of the schools under supervising principals.

VII. The introduction of cooking classes in the Normal School.

VIII. The exhibition of school work in Horticultural Hall.

IX. The assumption by the Board of Education of the kindergarten schools.

X. The establishment of the Chair of Pedagogy in the University of Pennsylvania.

XI. The lectures in Pedagogy in the Summer School of the Extension Society.

XII. The separation of the Girls' High and Normal Schools and the material improvement of the courses in the former.

XIII. The passage of the Compulsory School Law.

The Association encouraged and assisted all of these movements; it initiated and completed some of them. There are still other tasks for the Association. The new Compulsory School Law will render a school census necessary. The school accommodations of the city will be inadequate to meet the requirements of the law, and the enforcement of the law itself will depend upon public sentiment. In all these matters the Society can be of assistance.

The Department of Education should be reorganized. The Association has already made strenuous efforts to have the sectional boards abolished, and it seemed at times as if the measure would pass the Legislature. The agitation should be continued until the Department of Education is placed beyond the reach of politics. The administration of the city schools should be committed to a single body. These are some of the subjects which should receive the attention of the Association. The work of the Public Education Association is not completed. The educational welfare of so large a municipality as Philadelphia will require the continued aid of this influential organization, which in the past has accomplished so much for the advancement of the schools.

APPENDIX I.

OFFICERS OF THE PUBLIC EDUCATION ASSOCIATION FROM 1882 TO 1896.

1882.
Chairman.
JAMES S. WHITNEY.

Treasurer.
DALTON DORR.

Secretary.
MISS PENDLETON.

1883.
Chairman.
JAMES S. WHITNEY.

Treasurer.
DALTON DORR.

Secretary.
MISS PENDLETON.

1884.
Chairman.
JAMES S. WHITNEY.

Corresponding Secretary.
MISS PENDLETON.

Treasurer.
MRS. J. DUNDAS LIPPINCOTT.

Recording Secretary.
WILLIAM W. JUSTICE.

1885.
Chairman.
JAMES S. WHITNEY.

Corresponding Secretary.
MISS PENDLETON.

Treasurer.
MRS. J. DUNDAS LIPPINCOTT.

Recording Secretary.
WILLIAM W. JUSTICE.

1886—1890.
Chairman.
WILLIAM W. JUSTICE.

Corresponding Secretary.
MISS PENDLETON.

Treasurer.
MRS. J. DUNDAS LIPPINCOTT.

Recording Secretary.
WILLIAM W. WILTBANK.

1891.
Chairman.
————

Corresponding Secretary.
MISS PENDLETON.

Treasurer.
MRS. J. DUNDAS LIPPINCOTT.

Recording Secretary.
WILLIAM W. WILTBANK.

1892.
Chairman.
————

Corresponding Secretary.
MISS PENDLETON.

Treasurer.
MRS. J. DUNDAS LIPPINCOTT.

Recording Secretary.
WILLIAM W. WILTBANK.

1893.
Chairman.
EDMUND J. JAMES.

Corresponding Secretary.
MISS PENDLETON.

Treasurer.
MRS. J. DUNDAS LIPPINCOTT.

Recording Secretary.
WILLIAM W. WILTBANK.

1894.
Chairman.
EDMUND J. JAMES.

Treasurer.
MRS. J. DUNDAS LIPPINCOTT.

Recording Secretary.
WILLIAM W. WILTBANK.

1895.
Chairman.
EDMUND J. JAMES.

Treasurer.
MISS E. W. JANNEY.

Recording Secretary.
WILLIAM W. WILTBANK.

The following persons have served on the various committees of the Public Education Association :

COMMITTEE OF CONFERENCE WITH THE BOARD OF EDUCATION.

JAMES S. WHITNEY,
HON. GEO. W. HALL,

PHILIP C. GARRETT,
EDWARD SHIPPEN,

E. COPPÉE MITCHELL,
ROBERT E. PATTISON,

DALTON DORR.

COMMITTEE ON LAWS.

EDWARD SHIPPEN,

MISS PENDLETON,
WM. W. WILTBANK,
DALLAS SANDERS,
PHILIP C. GARRETT,

HENRY REED,
FRANCIS RAWLE,
WAYNE MACVEAGH,
A. SYDNEY BIDDLE.

COMMITTEE ON SCHOOLS.

E. COPPÉE MITCHELL,

MRS. MUMFORD,
MRS. U. C. HEAD,
MISS FLORENCE KELLY,
MISS CORNELIA HANCOCK,

MISS ANNA HALLOWELL,
LOUIS WAGNER,
MISS PENDLETON,
MRS. GILLINGHAM.

COMMITTEE ON KINDERGARTENS.

W. W. JUSTICE,
MRS. HARE,

MRS. MUMFORD,
PHILIP C. GARRETT.

COMMITTEE ON HOUSEHOLD ECONOMY.

MISS PENDLETON,
MRS. LIPPINCOTT,

MRS. MUMFORD,
MISS MEREDITH.

CORRESPONDING MEMBERS.

EDWARD T. STEEL,
DR. WILLIAM HARRIS,
MISS LUCRETIA P. HALE,
GEORGE WILLIAM CURTIS,
MISS THOMAS,
PROFESSOR J. M. ORDWAY,
CHARLES FRANCIS ADAMS, JR.,
M'LLE MATILDE DEMMLER,
PRESIDENT D. C. GILMAN,
PROFESSOR G. STANLEY HALL,
GEORGE W. FETTER,
WILLIAM L. SAYRE,

PROFESSOR M. B. SNYDER,
JAMES MAC ALISTER,
ANDREW J. MORRISON,
JAMES F. C. SICKEL,
MISS LYDIA A. KIRBY,
MISS MARY HAGGENBOTHAM,
DR. FRANKLIN TAYLOR,
EDGAR A. SINGER,
H. W. HALLIWELL,
HON. LOUIS BUSH,
PROFESSOR C. M. WOODWARD,
REV. I. L. LEUCHT,

E. A. BURKE.

APPENDIX II.

ANNUAL MEETINGS OF THE PUBLIC EDUCATION ASSOCIATION.

January 16, 1882.
January 13, 1883.
January 18, 1884.
January 26, 1885.
January 25, 1886.
January 22, 1887.
February 11, 1888.

February 21, 1889.
January 27, 1890.
April 20, 1891.
No Annual Meetings in 1892 and 1893.
March 9, 1894.
December 20, 1895.

Joint Meeting of the Public Education Association and the Civic Club, at the Galleries of the Art Club, March, 3, 1894.

APPENDIX III.

Abstract of the Treasurer's Reports.

This abstract is intended merely to show the sources of income and the purposes of expenditure of the Association. The full reports are printed in the Annual Reports of the Association.

JANUARY 13, 1883.

Subscriptions for 1882 and 1883	$48 00
Sundry payments made	4 50

JANUARY 18, 1884.
RECEIPTS.

Members' dues	$102 00
Subscriptions to lecture fund	390 00
	$535 00

EXPENDITURES.

Printing Annual Report	$67 01
Lecture course	356 20
Miscellaneous	77 41
	$500 62

JANUARY 26, 1885.
RECEIPTS.

Members' dues	$102 00
Subscriptions to lecture fund	167 85
	$304 73

EXPENDITURES.

For lectures.	$197 00
Printing reports	35 70
Sundry expenses	35 00
	$267 70

JANUARY 26, 1886.

RECEIPTS.

Members' dues for 1885 and 1886	$106 00
Subscriptions to lecture fund	50 00
	$192 78

EXPENDITURES.

For lectures	$112 45
Printing reports.	22 25
	$134 70

JANUARY 22, 1887.

RECEIPTS.

Annual subscriptions for 1886 and 1887	$138 00
Subscriptions to lecture fund	25 00
	$221 08

EXPENDITURES.

For lectures.	$19 87
Printing report	18 00
	$37 87

FEBRUARY 11, 1888.

RECEIPTS.

Annual subscriptions for 1887 and 1888	$246 00
Subscriptions to cooking fund	636 00
Cash from concert	866 29
	$1931 50

EXPENDITURES.

Printing Annual Report	$22 50
Paid toward cooking classes	900 00
	$922 50

JANUARY 29, 1889.

RECEIPTS.

Annual dues in 1888 and 1889	$84 00
Subscriptions to industrial exhibit	2270 00
Subscriptions to cooking fund	63 00
	$3426 00

EXPENDITURES.

Expense of annual meeting	$2 00
Paid toward cooking classes	800 00
Expenses of industrial exhibit	2216 56
	$3018 56

JANUARY 27, 1890.
RECEIPTS.

Annual dues	$250 00
Subscriptions to cooking fund	69 00
Donations to special appeal to cooking fund . . .	720 86
	$1447 30

EXPENDITURES.

Paid toward cooking classes	$955 00
Expense of manual training exhibit at Paris . . .	25 00
Printing scheme for Girls' High School	57 67
Stationery and printing	243 91
	$1281 58

APRIL 20, 1891.
RECEIPTS.

Subscriptions	$966 72

EXPENDITURES.

Cooking classes	$742 45
Printing	119 22
Subscription to chair of Pedagogy at University of Pennsylvania	250 00
	$1111 67

MARCH 9, 1894.
EXPENDITURES.

Pictures in Girls' Normal School	$100 00
Lectures at Summer School for Teachers	200 00
	$300 00

JANUARY 1, 1896.
RECEIPTS.

Annual dues	$228 00

EXPENDITURES.

Printing and postage	$ 81 69
Legal opinion and advice	50 00
Contribution in behalf of Education Bill before the Legislature	300 00
Rent of room	5 00
Alice Lippincott Memorial Room in the Alice Lippincott School	200 00

APPENDIX IV.

Hon. Robert Adams, Jr., 124 South Sixteenth Street, Philadelphia.

William C. Allison, Thirty-second and Walnut Streets, Philadelphia.

Rev. C. G. Ames, 1606 Mount Vernon Street, Philadelphia.

Mrs. C. G. Ames, 1606 Mount Vernon Street, Philadelphia.

Charles B. Baeder, 730 Market Street, Philadelphia.

Mrs. Matthew Baird, Merion Station, Mantgomery County.

John Baird, 214 South Twenty-fourth Street, Philadelphia.

Mrs. E. W. Balch, 1412 Spruce Street, Philadelphia.

Charles H. Banes, Market Street National Bank, Philadelphia.

George W. Banks, Twelfth and Chestnut Streets, Philadelphia.

Wharton Barker, 28 South Third Street, Philadelphia.

A. Sydney Biddle, 1224 Spruce Street, Philadelphia.

Cadwalader Biddle, 208 South Fourth Street, Philadelphia.

Hon. Craig Biddle, 2033 Pine Street, Philadelphia.

Mrs. George Biddle, 312 South Twelfth Street, Philadelphia.

Mrs. Arthur Biddle, 1822 De Lancey Place, Philadelphia.

Alexander Biddle, 1307 Walnut Street, Philadelphia.

Clement M. Biddle, Lansdowne.

Miss Biswanger, 1710 Oxford Street, Philadelphia.

Mrs. A. Blair, Southeast Corner Sixteenth and Sansom Streets, Philadelphia.

Mrs. Andrew A. Blair, 1802 De Lancey Place, Philadelphia.

Rudolph Blankenburg, 1326 Arch Street, Philadelphia.

Mrs. L. Lucretia Blankenburg, 1326 Arch Street, Philadelphia.

Rachel L. Bodley, M. D., 1400 North Twenty-first Street, Philadelphia.

Wendell P. Bowman, 130 South Sixth Street, Philadelphia.

Joseph H. Bromley, 127 Susquehanna Avenue, Philadelphia.

Dr. Edward Brooks, 713 Filbert Street, Philadelphia.

T. Wistar Brown, Villanova.

Alexander Brown, Nineteenth and Walnut Streets, Philadelphia.

Conyers Button, Germantown, Philadelphia.

Addison B. Burk, *Ledger* Office, Philadelphia.

William Burnham, 220 South Fourth Street, Philadelphia.

' Arthur M. Burton, 1512 Spruce Street, Philadelphia.

Charles Cadwalader, M. D., 240 South Fourth Street, Philadelphia.

John Cadwalader, 1518 Locust Street, Philadelphia.

J. Albert Caldwell, 1531 Pine Street, Philadelphia.

William T. Carter, 302 Walnut Street, Philadelphia.

Miss Frances Case, 1334 Spruce Street, Philadelphia.

John H. Catherwood, 50 South Front Street, Philadelphia.

Miss Clark, 2008 De Lancey Place, Philadelphia.

Clarence H. Clark, Forty-second and Locust Streets, Philadelphia.

E. W. Clark, Bullitt Building, Fourth Street, Philadelphia.

Clarence M. Clark, Jr., Ross and Mill Streets, Germantown, Philadelphia.

Richard A. Cleeman, M. D., 340 South Twenty-first Street, Philadelphia.

Isaac H. Clothier, 801 Market Street, Philadelphia.

George M. Coates, 127 Market Street, Philadelphia.

A. M. Collins, 527 Arch Street, Philadelphia.

Mrs. W. D. Comegys, Chestnut Hill, Philadelphia.

Howard Comfort, 529 Arch Street, Philadelphia.

John H. Converse, 500 North Broad Street, Philadelphia.

Mrs. Walter Cope, Main Street, Corner Upsal, Germantown, Philadelphia.

John F. Craig, 143 South Front Street, Philadelphia.

William P. Cresson, 224 South Broad Street, Philadelphia.

Miss Ida Cushman, 1340 Walnut Street, Philadelphia.

Miss Alice Cushman, 1340 Walnut Street, Philadelphia.

Francis T. S. Darley, 1118 Chestnut Street, Philadelphia.

Eugene Delano, Fourth and Chestnut Streets, Philadelphia.
Mrs. Samuel Dickson, 901 Clinton Street, Philadelphia.
Charles T. Dissel, 3307 Arch Street, Philadelphia.
Hamilton Disston, Broad and Jefferson Streets, Philadelphia.
Thomas Dolan, Hancock and Oxford Streets, Philadelphia.
Dalton Dorr, 2104 Locust Street, Philadelphia.
Anthony J. Drexel, 34 South Third Street, Philadelphia.

J. L. Erringer, Manheim Street, Germantown, Philadelphia.
Lincoln L. Eyre, 315 South Sixteenth Street, Philadelphia.

George H. Fisher, 1311 Locust Street, Philadelphia.
Hon. Edwin H. Fitler, 23 North Water Street, Philadelphia.
Simon Fleisher, 2030 Green Street, Philadelphia.
William G. Foulke, Wayne Street, Germantown, Philadelphia.
W. W. Frazier, Front and Chestnut Streets, Philadelphia.
Miss Cornelia Frothingham, 2035 Walnut Street, Philadelphia.
Dr. W. H. Furness, 1429 Pine Street, Philadelphia.

Philip C. Garrett, Logan Station, Philadelphia.
Henry C. Gibson, 1612 Walnut Street, Philadelphia.
Mrs. E. D. Gillespie, 250 South Twenty-first Street, Philadelphia.
James M. Gillilan, 1613 Walnut Street, Philadelphia.
Mrs. W. J. Gillingham, 973 North Eleventh Street, Philadelphia.
J. E. Gillingham, 311 Walnut Street, Philadelphia.
Stephen Greene, 27 South Fifth Street, Philadelphia.
Thomas H. Green, 731 Chestnut Street, Philadelphia.
Clement A. Griscom, 307 Walnut Street, Philadelphia.

Miss Buelah M. Hacker, 116 South Twenty-second Street, Philadelphia.
Daniel Haddock, Jr., 806 Pine Street, Philadelphia.
Hon. George W. Hall, 1131 Arch Street, Philadelphia.
A. R. Hall, 709 Market Street, Philadelphia.

Mrs. Edwin L. Hall, 3919 Spruce Street, Philadelphia.

Miss Anna Hallowell, 908 Clinton Street, Philadelphia.

Miss Emily Hallowell, 908 Clinton Street, Philadelphia.

Miss Cornelia Hancock, 309 Branch Street, Philadelphia

Mrs. Robert Harford Hare, 2031 De Lancey Place, Philadelphia.

Hon. J. I. Clark Hare, 118 South Twenty-second Street, Philadelphia.

Joseph S. Harris, School Lane, Germantown, Philadelphia.

Mrs. Alfred C. Harrison, 1616 Locust Street, Philadelphia.

Byerly Hart, 108 South Twenty-first Street, Philadelphia.

Mrs. Elizabeth S. Head, Green Street, Germantown, Philadelphia.

Morton P. Henry, 2200 St. James Place, Philadelphia.

Miss Addie S. Hover, 713 Filbert Street, Philadelphia.

Dr. Herbert M. Howe, 1606 Locust Street, Philadelphia.

Charles A. Hutchinson, 1617 Walnut Street, Philadelphia.

Professor James Hyslope, Columbia College, New York City.

Miss Irwin, 1834 Spruce Street, Philadelphia.

Dr. Louis Jack, 1533 Locust Street, Philadelphia.

Professor E. J. James, University of Pennsylvania, Philadelphia.

Miss Janney, Ogontz, Pennsylvania.

Dr. M. Jastrow, 65 West Upsal Street, Philadelphia.

H. L. Jayne, Nineteenth and Chestnut Streets, Philadelphia.

Dr. Horace Jayne, University of Pennsylvania, Philadelphia.

Dr. E. C. Jayne, 242 Chestnut Street, Philadelphia.

William W. Justice, Manheim Street, Germantown, Philadelphia.

Dr. W. W. Keen, 1729 Chestnut Street, Philadelphia.

Miss Florence Kelly, New Century Club, Philadelphia.

Hon. Joseph P. Kennedy, 209 South Sixth Street, Philadelphia.

Mrs. George W. Kendrick, Jr., 3507 Baring Street, Philadelphia.

Franklin Kirkbride, 1406 Spruce Street, Philadelphia.

Edward C. Knight, Water and Chestnut Streets, Philadelphia.

R. Koradi, 1502 Green Street, Philadelphia.

———

Henry C. Lea, 2000 Walnut Street, Philadelphia.

Dr. Philip Leidy, 526 Marshall Street, Philadelphia.

Charles Godfrey Leland, 220 South Broad Street, Philadelphia.

Edward Lewis, Cor. Thirty-third Street and Powelton Avenue, Philadelphia.

Dr. F. W. Lewis, 2016 Spruce Street, Philadelphia.

Enoch Lewis, 233 South Fourth Street, Philadelphia.

Mrs. Dundas Lippincott, 509 South Broad Street, Philadelphia.

Mrs. Joshua Lippincott, 1333 Walnut Street, Philadelphia.

J. Dundas Lippincott, 400 Locust Street, Philadelphia.

E. Dunbar Lockwood, 251 South Third Street, Philadelphia.

James Long, Union Trust Company, Philadelphia.

Morris Longstreth, M. D., 1416 Spruce Street, Philadelphia.

Colonel William Ludlow, 2215 St. James Place, Philadelphia.

Mrs. Charles M. Lukens, East Walnut Lane, Germantown, Philadelphia.

———

Thomas MacKellar, 606 Sansom Street, Philadelphia.

Wayne MacVeagh, 1603 Locust Street, Philadelphia.

Mrs. John Markoe, 2011 Pine Street, Philadelphia.

Richard S. Mason, School Lane, Germantown, Philadelphia.

Rev. Joseph May, 1306 Pine Street, Philadelphia.

H. Pratt McKean, 1923 Walnut Street, Philadelphia.

Miss Meredith, 233 South Thirteenth Street, Philadelphia.

H. W. Middleton, 945 Ridge Avenue, Philadelphia.

C. W. Middleton, 945 Ridge Avenue, Philadelphia.

L. W. Miller, 1709 Chestnut Street, Philadelphia.

E. Coppée Mitchell, 518 Walnut Street, Philadelphia.

Mrs. Lucretia M. B. Mitchell, 5012 Elm Avenue, Philadelphia.

Miss Morais, 546 North Fifth Street, Philadelphia.

Mrs. Mumford, 1401 North Seventeenth Street, Philadelphia.

J. P. Mumford, Bank of the Republic, Philadelphia.

John Mundell, 119 North Thirteenth Street, Philadelphia.

Nathan Myers, 426 Walnut Street, Philadelphia.

———

Miss Pauline Neidhard, 1511 Arch Street, Philadelphia.

George M. Newhall, 225 Church Street, Philadelphia.

Isaac Norris, M. D., 1424 Walnut Street, Philadelphia.

———

S. Davis Page, 289 South Fourth Street, Philadelphia.

Hon. Robert E. Pattison, Overbrook, Philadelphia.

James W. Paul, Jr., Fifth and Chestnut Streets, Philadelphia.

Judge William S. Peirce, 1032 Spruce Street, Philadelphia.

Miss Pendleton, 1522 Locust Street, Philadelphia.

William Pepper, M. D., 1811 Spruce Street, Philadelphia.

Hon. Boies Penrose, 1331 Spruce Street, Philadelphia.

Charles Platt, 232 Walnut Street, Philadelphia.

Charles E. Pugh, 233 South Fourth Street, Philadelphia.

———

Robert Ralston, 233 South Thirteenth Street, Philadelphia.

Francis Rawle, 402 Walnut Street, Philadelphia.

Henry Reed, Northeast Corner Eighteenth and Spruce Streets, Philadelphia.

Charles D. Reed, 261 North Sixth Street, Philadelphia.

Professor G. I. Riche, Central High School, Philadelphia.

George B. Roberts, 233 South Fourth Street, Philadelphia.

Miss Robins, 1110 Spruce Street, Philadelphia.

Joseph G. Rosengarten, 1532 Chestnut Street, Philadelphia.

———

Dallas Sanders, 410 South Fifteenth Street, Philadelphia.

Miss Emily Sartain, 1346 North Broad Street, Philadelphia.

Coleman Sellers, 3301 Baring Street, Philadelphia.

William Sellers, 1600 Hamilton Street, Philadelphia.

J. B. Sheppard, Jr., 2019 Arch Street, Philadelphia.
Edward Shippen, 532 Walnut Street, Philadelphia.
Miss Shoemaker, Fifteenth and Race Streets, Philadelphia.
William M. Singerly, *Record* Building, Philadelphia.
Andrew J. Sloan, 1012 Chestnut Street, Philadelphia.
Charles Smith, 303 Chestnut Street, Philadelphia.
Charles E. Smith, 702 Chestnut Street, Philadelphia.
Joseph P. Sinnott, 4228 Chestnut Street, Philadelphia.
Lindley Smyth, 431 Chestnut Street, Philadelphia.
James Spear, 1014 Market Street, Philadelphia.
Henry M. Steel, McKean Avenue, Germantown, Philadelphia.
Daniel Steinmetz, 501 Commerce Street, Philadelphia.
Samuel Sternberger, 720 North Twentieth Street, Philadelphia.
John S. Stevens, 3913 Walnut Street, Philadelphia.
Mrs. Cornelius Stevenson, 124 South Twenty-third Street, Philadelphia.
J. C. Strawbridge, Eighth and Market Streets, Philadelphia.

George C. Thomas, Fifth and Chestnut Streets, Philadelphia.
Professor R. E. Thompson, Central High School, Philadelphia.
Samuel G. Thompson, 1630 Spruce Street, Philadelphia.
Henry Tilge, 306 New Street, Philadelphia.
Charlemagne Tower, 228 South Seventh Street, Philadelphia.
George M. Troutman, 109 South Fourth Street, Philadelphia.

C. E. Vollmer, 628 North Tenth Street, Philadelphia.
A. W. Von Utassy, Green and Harvey Streets, Germantown, Philadelphia.

Samuel Wagner, 251 South Fourth Street, Philadelphia.
Louis Wagner, 218 Walnut Street, Philadelphia.
W. G. Warden, School Lane, Germantown, Philadelphia.
Redwood Warner, School Lane, Germantown, Philadelphia.
William Waterall, 200 North Fourth Street, Philadelphia.
Miss Edith Wetherill, 1413 Spruce Street, Philadelphia.
C. N. Weygandt, 124 Tulpehocken Street, Germantown, Philadelphia.

Mrs. Charles Wheeler, Walnut Street, below Nineteenth, Philadelphia.

James Whitall, 9 East Penn Street, Germantown, Philadelphia.

Dr. J. William White, 218 South Sixteenth Street, Philadelphia.

James S. Whitney, 1815 Vine Street, Philadelphia.

Mrs. James S. Whitney, 1815 Vine Street, Philadelphia.

William B. Whitney, East Walnut Lane, Germantown, Philadelphia.

Ellis D. Williams, 323 Walnut Street, Philadelphia.

Albert B. Williams, 323 Walnut Street, Philadelphia.

Hon. H. W. Williams, Supreme Court of Pennsylvania.

Talcott Williams, 331 South Sixteenth Street, Philadelphia.

Mrs. Talcott Williams, 331 South Sixteenth Street, Philadelphia.

I. V. Williamson, 30 Bank Street, Philadelphia.

De Forrest Willard, M. D., 1601 Walnut Street, Philadelphia.

William W. Wiltbank, 400 Chestnut Street, Philadelphia.

W. Macpherson Wiltbank, 400 Chestnut Street, Philadelphia.

David S. Wiltberger, 1612 Wallace Street, Philadelphia.

Henry Winsor, 338 South Delaware Avenue, Philadelphia.

Mrs. Owen Jones Wister, Butler Place, Green Lane Station.

Mrs. Caspar Wister, 1303 Arch Street, Philadelphia.

Langhorne Wister, 257 South Fourth Street, Philadelphia.

Dillwyn Wister, 4763 Wayne Avenue, Germantown, Philadelphia.

Miss Mary C. Wister, 1007 Spruce Street, Philadelphia.

Stuart Wood, 400 Chestnut Street, Philadelphia.

Walter Wood, 400 Chestnut Street, Philadelphia.

George Wood, 1239 North Broad Street, Philadelphia.

Richard Wood, 1620 Locust Street, Philadelphia.

James A. Wright, 305 Walnut Street, Philadelphia.

F. Stuart Wyeth, 1511 Locust Street, Philadelphia.

F. H. Wyeth, 1912 Locust Street, Philadelphia.